Linda Viner studied archaeology at Leicester University, her choice of subject inspired by the landscape of the Berkshire Downs and the countless walks and family picnics exploring Wayland's Smithy and the Uffington White Horse.

A life-long interest in landscape archaeology, local history and the countryside in general, both natural and man-made, has ensured that the shortest journey or the longest holiday is never boring. And Dorset could be nothing but inspiring.

Following page
The ruins of the isolated medieval church of Knowlton stand within the banks of a prehistoric henge monument. The earthworks of the depopulated medieval village lie 600 yards to the north on the banks of the River Allen, a close neighbour to the deserted village of Brockington.

DISCOVER DORSET

LOST VILLAGES

LINDA VINER

THE DOVECOTE PRESS

The Depopulated Village
As oft I see by sight, or oft
In mind, the ridges on the ground,
The mark of many a little croft
And house where now no wall is found,
I call the folk to life again
And build their houses up anew;
I ween I shape them wrong, but who
Can now outmark their shapes to men?
WILLIAM BARNES

The church at Knowlton.

First published in 2002 by The Dovecote Press Ltd
Stanbridge, Wimborne, Dorset BH21 4JD

ISBN 1 874336 95 4

Series designed by Humphrey Stone

Typeset in Monotype Sabon
Printed and bound by Baskerville Press, Salisbury, Wiltshire

A CIP catalogue record for this book is available
from the British Library

3 5 7 9 8 6 4 2

CONTENTS

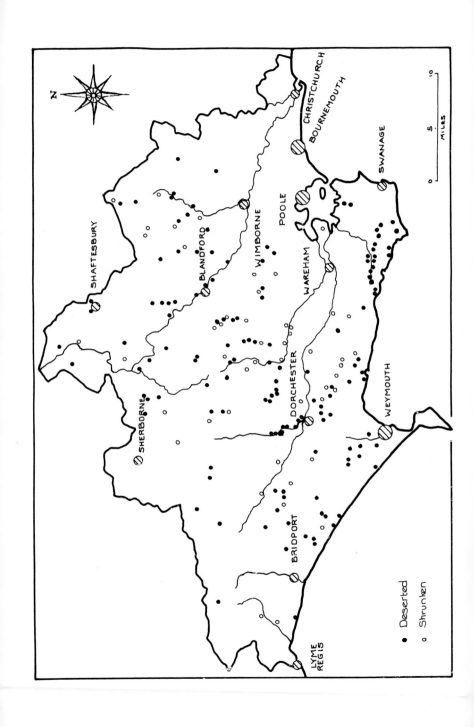

INTRODUCTION

Most people, if asked to define the elements which go to make up a village, would describe a group of houses and farms, clustered around a church and manor house, with a rectory or vicarage, and perhaps a chapel, pub, shop and school – a self-contained rural community with, until recently, many of its residents earning their living from agriculture.

Dorset is studded with innumerable village gems. They are the survivors. But what of those that are 'lost'? For many, Tyneham would have to be the archetypal 'lost village', a village suspended in time. On a visit today it is comparatively easy to visualize the village in its heyday, over sixty years ago. Memories and photographs enhance the personal experience of many visitors who still live in the countryside themselves, or whose parents or grandparents have recounted their tales of rural life before flushing toilets, electricity, television and the Internet. The walls may only survive as stubs but it is still possible to wander the village street and recognize the individual character of each house and feel at home in the surroundings.

To visit a medieval 'lost village' demands more imagination and often the eye of faith, aided and abetted by a host of tools and guides supplied by landscape archaeologists and local historians. Bardolfeston is the classic medieval 'lost village' in Dorset. As at Tyneham, the village is there for all to see with its street, houses and gardens, but it survives as a series of humps and bumps in a grassy field. Once recognised for what they are, and set within the broader pattern of fields and trackways, it is possible to appreciate the footprint left by the many lost villages, hamlets and farms which now dot the Dorset landscape.

Map showing the pattern of deserted and shrunken villages in the county, reflecting the fieldwork of Ronald Good, Christopher Taylor, Alan Hunt and other landscape historians.

LOST VILLAGES

In England, between 1300 and 1500, over three thousand villages disappeared, and countless others were reduced in size. The areas worst affected lay in a broad band across the Midland counties of Northamptonshire, Warwickshire and Worcestershire, and stretched as far south as Wiltshire and into Dorset.

These late medieval desertions were just one episode in a long and complicated sequence of settlement history. Villages have always mutated, developing and decaying in a constantly shifting landscape, within a time span stretching over hundreds of years. The reasons for the rapid increase in the number of abandoned villages are many and complex, and the Black Death of 1348-9 is not the sole culprit, despite its place in popular tradition.

Throughout the centuries various factors have contributed to the loss of communities, while others prospered and developed at the expense of their weaker neighbours. The poem by the great Dorset dialect poet, William Barnes, the first verse of which fittingly begins this book, shows how touched he was by the plight of the landless labourer, evicted as a result of nineteenth-century enclosures.

Rural depopulation is a process which continues to this day in the guise of holiday cottages and second homes. In the twenty-first century how many villages could be classed as 'lost', especially in the winter months?

Loss is an emotive word, highly charged and full of sorrow, an emotion experienced as much by the villagers of Milton Abbas in the 1770s who were moved to a model village out of sight of the big house, as those of Tyneham, ordered in 1943 to relinquish their homes with the promise, so far unfulfilled, that one day they would be allowed to return.

Only a spattering of former settlements are truly 'lost', unrecorded in documents, invisible on the ground, or undetected because of

Milton Abbey and the mansion built by Lord Milton, photographed in 1950. Between 1770 and 1776 about 100 houses, 3 inns, a school and almshouses were swept away to provide Lord Milton with privacy and parkland. Much of the old town now lies beneath the lake to the east of the abbey.

human failing to appreciate their presence in the landscape. The majority have left an imprint of their former selves - a tantalising reference in a tax return, a place-name, an isolated church, a parchmark in pasture during a hot summer, a scatter of pottery, or humps and bumps in a field.

The pioneering study of lost villages by Maurice Beresford, *The Lost Villages of England* (1954), listed 19 sites in Dorset. By 1971, that figure had risen to 42, including West Bexington, Bryanston, Frome Belet, Milton Abbas, West Ringstead, Stanton St Gabriel, Winterborne Came and Winterborne Farringdon.

For such sites the 'lost' element was initially recognised from documentary research of medieval records which showed that former villagers had dutifully paid their taxes, but to visit the village today would be frustrating, despite being armed with the relevant Ordnance Survey map. The village had disappeared - apparently. By combining documentary research and archaeological fieldwork it was possible to recognise the gaps in the settlement pattern of a particular area. From concentrating on one missing element, the study of deserted villages has evolved to attempt to disentangle and understand the total landscape and the relationships between neighbouring settlement types, the field systems which sustained each community and the changing fortunes of each through time.

Landscape archaeology draws upon the skills of geographers, historians, cartographers, archaeologists, photographers, vernacular architects, surveyors, ecologists and natural scientists. In 1954 Maurice Beresford estimated that there were 1353 deserted medieval villages in England. Through the efforts of the Deserted Medieval Village Research Group (now the Medieval Settlement Research Group) the total had risen to 2813 in 1976, and in 2000 was over 3000.

For Dorset, Ronald Good's book, *The Lost Villages of Dorset* (1979), was the first to draw together all the scattered references 'about the ways in which the rural settlements in the county have waxed and waned in size and local importance with the passage of the years'. Professor Good listed 36 truly 'lost' villages, 26 where the village was replaced by a country house, and 85 now represented only by a single farmstead. In separate categories he noted 29 villages which had undergone change, principally as a result of settlement shift or shrinkage, and 45 place-names which were 'not precisely identified' but were indicative of former settlement.

In recent years additional survey work has increased the total to at least 254 sites of either deserted or shrunken settlements in the county. Many more still lie unrecorded. There are far too many to describe individually within the scope of this book, but it is hoped that a chosen few will highlight the clues present in the landscape and lead to an appreciation of the many which pepper the county.

For those not inclined to weather the great outdoors, documents deposited in record offices, reference libraries and museums can be

Judge Wyndham's Oak, seen here from Silton churchyard, marks the centre of the village, which was probably abandoned following the enclosure of the open fields after the manor was bought by Sir Hugh Wyndham in the seventeenth century.

equally valuable. Maps offer an opportunity to trace the development of the settlement pattern on a county-wide scale and at the focused parish level. Early parish and estate maps, and Tithe and Enclosure maps, all provide a framework from which to develop further research. Dorset is extremely fortunate in its early cartographic coverage, particularly the large-scale map of the county surveyed by Isaac Taylor in 1765.

Early Ordnance Survey maps, especially the first edition 1-inch to the mile surveyed in 1811 and the 6-inch survey published in the 1880's, are essential aids. The more recent Explorer and Outdoor Leisure OS maps follow a policy of marking historical sites: 'Earthworks' or 'Village Earthworks' at Rew, West Bexington, Whitcombe, Broadmayne, Warmwell; 'Medieval Village (site of)' for

Listed as part of 'Tatetun' in Domesday Book, Tatton Farm (Chickerell) occupies the site of East Tatton which was formerly in Buckland Ripers parish (looking north).

Modbury, Winterborne Farringdon, Elston, West Ringstead and Wolfeton for example. But please note: map inscription does not imply public access.

Place-names and field-names can be useful indicators of the earlier pattern of settlement and land use. Names ending in 'wick', 'cote', 'worth' or 'ton' may help to pinpoint former sites as at Hethfelton, Hemsworth, and Holworth. Changes in spelling can often mask or disguise the early origin of a name, as in the case of Dibberford in Broadwinsor parish which in the eleventh century was spelt 'Dibberwurthe', meaning the 'enclosure belonging to a man called Dycgbeorht'. Many field-names recorded on nineteenth-century tithe maps, such as Church Close, Town Field, Town End, Township Field, and Boon's Field, can offer a pointer to the potential sites of former farmsteads, hamlets or villages.

Documents provide one of the primary sources for contemporary references to villages when they were either still occupied or were on the point of being deserted. The majority of the earliest sources are estate and manor court records and surveys, compiled by government, church and manor officials to assess taxes, rents and rates. Desertion was often a long drawn-out process, but the Lay Subsidies and Poll Taxes of the fourteenth century and the Hearth Taxes of the 1660s and 1670s can pinpoint the moment when villages disappear from the record. Errors, evasions, and omissions cloud the fiscal and economic returns, but, with care, the general trends of prosperity and decline can be appreciated. The documents touch upon the lives of ordinary men and women and on occasion allow us to 'people' the villages with named individuals.

County historians such as Gerard and Hutchins, and travellers such as Leland and Defoe are a source for topographical descriptions and personal accounts of the contemporary scene. One early record of depopulation is provided by John Leland, a noted antiquarian and traveller throughout Tudor England. Of Portland he wrote, 'At the present time [1542] there are about eighty houses on the island, although ruins suggest that there were once nearly twice as many. There is only one street of houses; the remainder are scattered . . .'.

The development of aerial photography in the last fifty years has literally expanded our horizons and transformed the confused ground level pattern of low banks and random stretches of hollow-ways to give a bird's-eye view of the houses and main street of the former village. Oblique photographs provide the broader view, while vertical photographs can be used to map individual features such as house sites. Both allow the village to be set in relation to the wider landscape of fields, trackways, and neighbouring settlements.

Aerial photographs taken in the 1940s are now an invaluable record of sites, many of which have since been degraded due to ploughing, or have disappeared because of quarrying, house building, or deliberate destruction. Where sites survive as upstanding earthworks shadows cast by low sun, or a light frost or snow cover, can accentuate the topography of a field under pasture. Dry hot summers can reveal the outline of stone foundations as parchmarks in pasture, or as cropmarks in cereal crops. Ploughing can disturb the vulnerable upper levels so that walls are represented by stone scatters spread across the surface of the field.

In recent years archaeological excavations and surveys have been

Medieval contemporary life can be glimpsed in the county's churches, perhaps most poignantly as here at Whitcombe, itself the site of a deserted village, where wall paintings show St Christopher carrying Christ.

undertaken at a number of sites. The first major excavation of a deserted medieval village in Dorset was carried out at Holworth in 1958. Since then settlements have been investigated at Owermoigne, West Bexington, Woolcombe in Toller Porcorum, and Ower Farm in Studland. Evaluations, surveys and fieldwalking have taken place at Witchampton, Compton Valence, Kingston Lacy and Lower Kingcombe, providing invaluable historical assessments of the broader landscape.

Excavations can reveal the stuff of daily life, providing tangible examples of the 'goods and chattells' listed in the wills and inventories of our forebears, and displayed in many local museums. But contemporary life can also be glimpsed in the medieval wall paintings and carved gargoyles, capitals and corbels to be found in many of the county's churches, most notably at Bere Regis, Cranborne, Tarrant Crawford, Wareham, Whitcombe and Studland.

RURAL SETTLEMENT

For many, the village is the quintessential focus of country living, but within the wider rural landscape it is just one element in a settlement hierarchy which includes hamlets and farmsteads, with associated features such as churches and manor houses, set in a jigsaw of fields, commons, heaths, parks and woodland, defined by field and estate boundaries and roads.

On the chalk the settlement pattern today is characterised by strings of villages with a church, manor house and cottages set along a single street running parallel to the river. Villages with a strong central core, whether it is based on the church or village green, are called 'nucleated' settlements by landscape historians. A common agricultural policy was the mainstay of the community, based upon the shared working of the large open fields and commons which surrounded the village. As a settlement type, villages are a late feature in the landscape and were not created until the late Anglo-Saxon or Viking period in the tenth century through to the twelfth century.

There are areas, especially on the clays and heaths of the county, where villages have never been the norm, and the dominant form of rural settlement has always been the hamlet or single farmstead, giving a dispersed pattern of settlement.

And there are hybrids where farmsteads represent secondary settle-ments in an area of predominantly nucleated villages. The landscape of farms and villages created by enclosure in the nineteenth century illustrates such a pattern, and mirrors the earlier colonisation of new land in the twelfth and thirteenth centuries in response to the increased demand for food made by a then rapidly expanding population.

Settlement history has always been fluid, with the village itself changing shape and size, and even location. And some disappear - or appear to. Within many villages gaps along the street frontage mark the plots of former houses, and earthworks in a field that separates the church from the village show that over time the settlement has shifted or contracted. This complex pattern of desertion and shrinkage underpins the way we look at the landscape today, and our understanding and appreciation of just why villages look the way they do, the changes that have gone on, and why a few failed.

Who owns which piece of land has always been of paramount importance, and the pattern of ownership, the act of enclosing space, is imprinted on the landscape in the form of walls, banks, hedges, and ditches. Many of the blocks of land defined by such boundaries existed long before they were first described in documents and many may have Roman or even late prehistoric origins.

The boundary clauses in charters of the late Saxon period describe features that were already well established in the landscape. Boundaries often follow natural features such as watercourses or hilltop ridges. Man-made structures such as barrows or other earthworks may be mentioned, or boundary stones survive to mark the course. The overall shape created may be significant. Short dog-leg stretches often indicate the former blocks of strips in the open fields. Odd protrusions or extensions may be the first indicator of the existence of a former settlement and detached fragments of parishes may exist as islands within another parish.

Estates or manors were important economic units. Owned by an individual or a corporate body such as a church or abbey, they were self-sufficient areas of land with a mixture of arable, meadow, wood and waste, over which the lord had certain rights and within which people lived and worked. Many had a single village focus, but equally the settlement pattern within an estate might comprise two or more villages, or a cluster of hamlets and a scatter of farmsteads.

From the late ninth century local lords founded churches centred on their estates. Many of the county's churches were built in the twelfth century, but they often occupy a site established as a religious focus in the tenth or eleventh century. The parish was a unit of pastoral care and was dependent on tithes to maintain the church fabric and its priest. It was only natural, therefore, for the parish boundary to follow that of the manorial estate and many parishes preserve the outline of the pre-Conquest land holdings.

Domesday Book, compiled in 1086, records the major

redistribution of land which took place after the Norman Conquest of 1066, when the Saxon landowners were ousted to be replaced by new Norman lords. The Crown was the largest single landowner, with William the Conqueror's half-brother Robert, the Count of Mortain, holding extensive estates throughout the county. The Bishop of Salisbury and the abbeys at Sherborne, Cerne, Milton and Abbotsbury and the nunnery at Shaftesbury were all well endowed, as were the many smaller religious houses.

It is important to emphasize that Domesday Book is a record of value, both of land and of people. It is not a list of villages per se, useful though it may be in many instances of providing the first documentary reference to an estate. But it does suggest a landscape already crowded with settlements.

Piddletrenthide is not a 'lost' village but, by extrapolation, an understanding of its complex tenurial holdings which are visible today can serve as a guide in identifying similar patterns elsewhere, many of which have either disappeared entirely, or survive as single farmsteads or earthworks. The modern village, strung out along the valley of the River Piddle, lies within a rectangular block of land, the boundaries of which were clearly defined by the tenth century. At Domesday the 'village' was assessed at thirty hides (a hide was 120 acres), hence its name, and a charter of 966 describes a single estate called Uppedelen, of ten hides, as a separate block of land occupying the northern third of the parish. An almost continuous hedge-line still demarcates its southern boundary, and a further long boundary divides the remaining two-thirds to create three separate land units. Prior to enclosure in 1817, each unit had its own common-field system, called Upper, Middle and Lower Tithing. The three settlements of Domesday can be identified today as the three separate groups of houses which make up the sprawling village: 'Uppiddle' centred on the church and manor house, a second group representing Middle Tithing, and Lower Tithing now called White Lackington.

Further south in the Piddle valley, Piddlehinton and Puddletown remain as large villages, but former settlements are strung out along the course of the river at Little Piddle, Combe Deverall, Muston, North and South Louvard, Waterston, Druce, and Bardolfeston. The settlement of Cheselbourne Ford, prior to its destruction in 1965,

Aerial photography provides a bird's-eye view of the earthworks of the deserted hamlet of North Louvard, lying in a field between Muston (bottom right) and Lea Farm (top left, looking south). The River Piddle marks the boundary between the parishes of Piddlehinton and Puddletown. Higher Waterston (top right) occupies the site of South Louvard

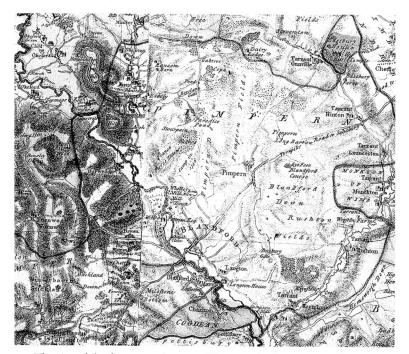

The site of the former settlement of Ranston in the Iwerne valley was mapped by Isaac Taylor in 1765 – his symbol for 'old foundations', resembling a four-petalled flower, drawn to the south of Ranston House. Hanford, Stepleton and Aish were also once much larger, while Lazerton, to the south of Stepleton, was already 'lost'.

survived as earthworks comprising a line of ten rectangular closes or paddocks on the bank of the Devil's Brook.

Similar strings of villages, both extant and lost, follow the watercourses of the Cerne, Frome, Tarrant, and north and south Winterborne rivers. Domesday Book is less than helpful in distinguishing between individual settlements by name and fieldwork is vital to disentangle the pattern on the ground.

In the Iwerne valley the parish settlements of Iwerne Minster, Iwerne Courtney (or Shroton), and Stourpaine survive while their earlier constituent elements of Preston, Ranston, Lazerton and Ash are now deserted or reduced to single houses or farms. The parish of Iwerne Stepleton survives today as a country house.

Ranston House, the village lay to the south of the house. The west front shown in the engraving was added to an earlier building in 1758 by Thomas Ryves.

Iwerne Courtney (Shroton) originally comprised three separate land units, centred on the present village, the hamlet of Farrington, and Ranston. At Domesday Ranston had a population of nine, and in 1274 five free tenants and ten villeins were listed. By 1662 only Ranston House remained, with the site of the village shown on Isaac Taylor's map by his symbol for 'old foundations', lying to the south of the eighteenth-century mansion (see illustration on previous page).

In the case of the modern parish of Charminster there were ten separate medieval land units: Charminster itself, Forston, Pulston, two un-named estates, Herrison, Cowden, Charlton, Wolfeton, and Burton. Wolfeton and Burton have earthworks which suggest shrinkage, while Pulston, Herrison and the two anonymous estates were deserted in the fourteenth and fifteenth centuries. The remains of the former farmstead of Charlton confirm it was never large and only one household was recorded 'atte Charleton Farme' in 1662. The earthworks cover about two acres, within a square enclosure, subdivided internally into five rectangular closes, with the possible remains of two house platforms visible in one corner. Ploughing in the past has produced pottery of the thirteenth to eighteenth centuries.

In the Tarrant valley twelve early land units are now represented by eight parishes. Fragmentary earthworks, as at Tarrant Launceston,

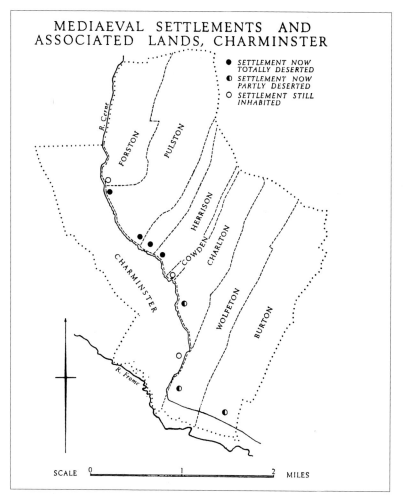

MEDIAEVAL SETTLEMENTS AND ASSOCIATED LANDS, CHARMINSTER

● SETTLEMENT NOW TOTALLY DESERTED
◐ SETTLEMENT NOW PARTLY DESERTED
○ SETTLEMENT STILL INHABITED

SCALE 0 ————————— 1 ————————————— 2 MILES

Extensive survey work by the Royal Commission on Historical Monuments has identified the early estates in the parish of Charminster, revealing the complex and dense pattern of settlements which once existed.

Tarrant Monkton and Tarrant Rawston, indicate more extensive areas of settlement in the past, while the eighteenth century creation of a park round Eastbury obliterated the medieval village of Tarrant Gunville. Few houses in Tarrant Rushton are earlier in date than the eighteenth century as the result of a disastrous fire recorded in the

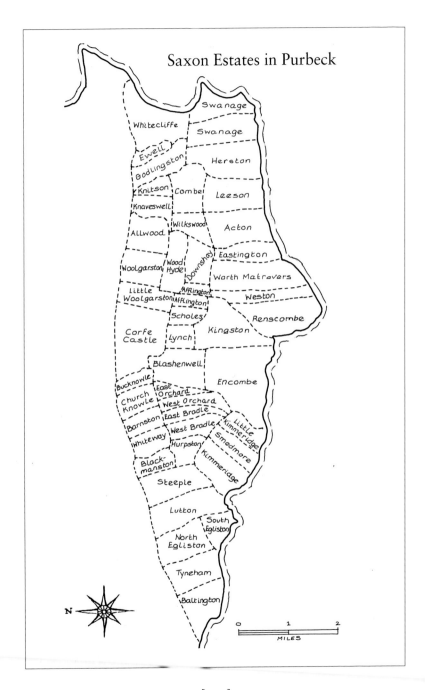

Saxon Estates in Purbeck

1664 Hearth Tax Returns, 'this tithing the dwelling houses were burnt down and not yet rebuilt'.

The Isle of Purbeck also exhibits an incredible complexity and density of settlements and early land units, and all are pre-Norman in origin. To the south of the Purbeck Hills, within the parishes of Tyneham, Steeple, Kimmeridge, Church Knowle, Corfe Castle, Worth Matravers, Langton Matravers, and Swanage there were at least forty individual land units. Their boundaries stretch across the hillsides as continuous hedgelines and many of the former settlements survive today as earthworks or as single farms or houses.

Tyneham is unique and will be described later, but within the parish there were settlements at Baltington, North and South Egliston; in Steeple, sites at Lutton, Hurpston, and Blackmanston; in Kimmeridge, sites at Smedmore, and Little Kimmeridge; in Church Knowle, sites at Whiteway, Barnston, Bucknowle, East Bradle, West Bradle, East and West Orchard; in Corfe Castle, sites at Little Woolgarston, Woolgarston, Ailwood, Blashenwell, Lynch, Scoles, Afflington, Encombe, and Kingston; in Worth Matravers, sites at Renscombe, Weston, Eastington, Wood Hyde, Downshay, and Afflington; in Langton Matravers, sites at Acton, Leeson, Coombe, Wilkswood, Knaveswell, and Knitson; and in Swanage, sites at Herston, Godlingston, and Whitecliff.

Encombe was one of the larger land units and remains a private estate today, centred around the imposing eighteenth-century mansion of Encombe House, set within landscaped grounds which include a sequence of lakes stretching down the valley towards the sea. A print entitled 'Chapel, Encombe' by Jean Claude Nattes (1765?-1822) has been pivotal in pinpointing the site of the earlier village, much of which must have been cleared during the landscaping of the grounds, but which was still visible at the time of Nattes' visit to the house.

The settlement pattern, particularly outside the chalk downlands, was and remains a loose conglomeration of farmsteads, set within irregularly-shaped fields.

Opposite page To the south of the Purbeck Hills, the intricate pattern of Saxon estates on the Isle of Purbeck is fossilised by the network of surviving field boundaries which demarcate the early land units.

The earthwork remains of the neighbouring settlements of East and West Bradle (Church Knowle) and Hurpston (Steeple), photographed in 1946 (north is at the bottom). Low sun highlights the rectangular closes to the north of Bradle Farm (centre) covering an area of about four acres, while Hurpston (to the right, represented by the single barn) was a small hamlet.

At the time of the Domesday Survey, the 'village' of Povington, to the north of the Purbeck Hills and now in Tyneham parish, was recorded as a manor of 8.5 hides with the demesne or manor farm worked by eight slaves, and with four villagers (villeins) and five smallholders (bordars) as tenants. Povington has never been a nucleated village and has always consisted of a group of scattered farmsteads. In 1815 there was one large farm of 230 acres, four smaller farms of 40-70 acres each, and eight to nine smallholdings each comprising a cottage with 5-15 acres of land. The dispersed settlement pattern was established by 1086, and has persisted through the centuries. Each farmstead was surrounded by its own irregularly-shaped enclosed fields, and there is no evidence for the open-field agriculture associated with nucleated villages.

In the Blackmore Vale, Marnhull today is a large scattered village within a maze of connecting lanes and footpaths, and with a complex history. It is not recorded in Domesday Book but was probably included within the entry for Sturminster Newton. It originally consisted of three separate settlements at Burton, Walton Elm and Kentleworth, but later building has gradually brought the three together.

Thornton, to the south-east, was a separate parish until the sixteenth century when it became part of Marnhull. It provides a good example of a class of settlement not often associated with Dorset, the moated site, where the farmhouse and outbuildings once sat within a water-filled moat. Others have been recorded in the parishes of Batcombe, Beaminster, Broadwindsor, Buckland Newton, Corscombe, Owermoigne, Shillingstone, Stourpaine and Tarrant Rushton. At Dewlish a moat formed one element within a larger pattern of linear earthworks to the south and east of the church which indicate either settlement shift or shrinkage within the village.

The earthworks in Court Close, to the south and east of the church at Dewlish (top right), are highlighted by low sun.
The remains of a rectangular moat (bottom right) suggest the possible site of a former manor house.

The inhabitants of Lyscombe were duty bound to send twelve trout each year to the Benedictine monks of Milton Abbey. Now sadly much decayed since this photograph was taken, the cottage on the right was the former twelfth-century chapel.

Side by side with the secular landlords, the power enjoyed by the bishops and the great Cistercian and Benedictine abbeys demonstrates the economic and political control enjoyed by the medieval church.

The Benedictine Houses at Milton, Abbotsbury, Cerne, Sherborne and Shaftesbury controlled large estates throughout the county. At the Dissolution in 1539 they left a legacy of prosperous villages and small towns, while the scale of their former wealth can be seen in the barns which survive at Abbotsbury, Cerne Abbas, and Sydling St Nicholas. Sheep were important not only for their wool, but also as providers of mutton, milk, cheese, and dung. Now, sadly in a sorry state of repair, the barn and chapel of a late medieval grange or farmstead survives at Lyscombe (Cheselbourne). It was formerly part of the Milton Abbey estates and local legend describes it as a chapel of ease for use by monks journeying between Milton and Cerne Abbeys. The inhabitants of Lyscombe were under an annual obligation to send twelve trout to the monks at Milton Abbey.

The Cistercians, in contrast, insisted on solitude and were prepared to transport themselves or move whole villages to achieve the required isolation demanded by their Order. Bindon Abbey was initially established in a remote corner of West Lulworth before moving to

Wool in 1172. Similarly, Forde Abbey (Thorncombe) was resettled in 1141, two miles from the village on the parish edge. Documentary evidence is lacking but it is most probable that the village of Tarrant Crawford was moved when one of the richest Cistercian nunneries in England was founded by Bishop Poore of Salisbury in 1230, adjacent to the original twelfth-century parish church on the banks of the River Tarrant. The village today is still largely deserted, and earthworks to the west of Crawford Farm mark the remains of former house sites.

The Bride Valley provided the ideal location for a grange farm for the Cistercian monks from Netley Abbey, near Southampton. The western gable of St Luke's Chapel survives at Ashley, on land originally given by William of Litton in return for the monks' perpetual prayers for himself and his family.

In the twelfth and thirteenth centuries population pressure resulted in the creation of new towns, hamlets and farmsteads, and the expansion of existing settlements, a process which Christopher Taylor has described as 'the filling up of the rural landscape'. The basic framework of settlement and land units had been established by the tenth century, and perhaps even earlier. Thereafter 'there was a continuous process of infilling of new settlement which went on until the mid thirteenth century in most places'.

The increase in the number and size of settlements is also reflected in the number of new boroughs created by the Crown. Not all, however, were successful and Gotowre or Newton (Studland) was the abortive 'new' town planned by Edward I on the Goathorn Peninsula. In 1286 Richard de Bosco and Walter de Marisco, a parson, were appointed to lay out a new town with a harbour having sufficient streets and lanes and adequate sites for a market and church and plots for merchants and others. Edward I's charter granted a twice-weekly market and an annual fair to the port which was intended to rival Poole. But it failed, and all is now hidden within forestry.

To feed the growing population the potential of all land was maximised: wet or marshy land was drained; assarts or clearings were made in waste and woodland; and strip lynchets were developed on steep hillsides to increase the land under arable cultivation.

The expansion of arable land in the twelfth and thirteenth centuries was part of a continuing process which Domesday Book records had already begun at Swyre in the eleventh century: land leased to Toxus (the priest?) was described, 'Previously it was pasture, now arable'. In 1314 Ingelman de Berenger, steward of Blackmoor Forest, was granted permission to 'reduce to cultivation' two separate areas of land at Hermitage, totalling 184 acres.

At the time of Domesday Stalbridge, in the Blackmore Vale, comprised two land units centred on Stalbridge and Stalbridge Weston, each with its own open field system, surrounded by forest and waste. Medieval documents suggest the gradual extension of arable land, with new settlements, mainly isolated farmsteads, establishing themselves on the periphery. The newly cleared land, or assarts, have typically irregularly-shaped fields enclosed by thick hedge banks. Farms and small settlements are first recorded at Gummershay Farm (1268), Marsh Farm (1327), Hargrove Farm (1268), Thornhill (1244), Antioch Farm (1244), Newnham (1244 - now lost) and Frith Farm (1244). Many may have even earlier origins, the result of expansion in Saxon times, but were not recorded in documents until centuries later.

Assarts in the wooded areas of the north and west were a feature mirrored by similar farm expansions in the south-east of the county. In Bere Regis, secondary settlements at Shitterton and Dodding's Farm were established on the chalk before the eleventh century. On the heathland to the south-east isolated farmsteads are first recorded in documents in the twelfth or thirteenth centuries, for example at Chamberlayne, Philliol, Stockley, and Hyde House. Again there is evidence, as at Hethfelton and Povington, that isolated farmsteads have much earlier origins than first expected.

Ridge and furrow which gives a field a corrugated look, so dominant a feature of the Midland counties, is an indicator of the former open-fields of a medieval village. Each village had two or three large fields for arable farming, growing crops of peas, beans, wheat, barley and oats. They were subdivided into narrow strips, each villager holding strips scattered within each large open field. The open-field system required a collective decision from all the villagers as to which crop was to be grown in which field each year. When it came time to cultivate the strips each plough team worked up one side of the strip, turned at the headland, and came down the other side.

In the parish of Portesham, farms now occupy the sites of East and West Shilvinghampton (left and right, looking south). Lower Farm (centre bottom) sits between the two older settlements which survive as a series of rectangular closes either side of sunken tracks which run north-south through the two villages.

The effect over time was to pile up the earth towards the middle of the strip, thus forming the ridge, leaving the hollow or furrow between neighbouring strips.

The thin light soils of the chalkland do not lend themselves to prominent ridges, but ridge and furrow survives at Winterborne Farringdon, Fifehead Magdalen, Hinton St Mary and Lydlinch. At Winterborne Houghton and Turnworth ridge and furrow has been found to overlie earlier prehistoric and Roman fields.

A rare survival of this medieval farming practice persists on Portland. Despite destruction by quarrying and modern building, blocks of individual strips survive, separated by earthen banks or drystone walls. A three-field or two-field rotation was in operation in the eight large open fields of South, Great West, Coomb, Droop or

Windmill, East, Court or Little West, Inmosthay and King Barrow. Pasture land was available at the extreme southern tip of the island or in the northern area around The Verne.

The pressure to increase the amount of land under arable cultivation extended the ploughed fields up the steeper slopes of the valleys, resulting in the development of strip lynchets as can be seen at Loders, Netherbury, Kimmeridge, Worth Matravers, Compton Abbas, Maiden Newton, and Bincombe.

To maintain fertility a period of fallow was essential. Temporary hurdles or fences enclosed blocks of arable land and sheep which were grazed on the higher ground were brought down and folded each night, their dung fertilising and enriching the soil. Thus a delicate balance between arable and pasture had to be struck, and any upset could spell disaster.

The population of England reached a peak of 5-6 million by the beginning of the fourteenth century and then began to decline, falling to 2-2.5 million by the end of the century. The reasons are many, and cannot be put down to one single factor. The population may have reached its limit of potential growth, given the economy, technology and agricultural practices of the time. The thin chalk soils were losing their fertility. Climatic change which heralded a series of wet summers and poor harvests in 1315, 1316 and 1321, with sheep and cattle murrains in 1313-17 and 1319-21, depleted stocks of cereals and animals, and led to starvation and malnutrition which by the 1330s had debilitated the peasant population.

The Tax Assessment in 1341-2, the Nonarum Inquisitiones or the Inquisitions of the Ninth, a levy of the ninth lamb, fleece and sheaf, records soil infertility and bad weather as reasons for the reduction of taxation liability for some villages.

And then, at the end of June 1348, came the Black Death, brought to England on a ship which docked at Melcombe Regis. Traditionally it has been blamed as the single devastating factor which ravaged the population of England, and has in popular folklore been used to explain the isolation of the churches at Lytchett Matravers and Knowlton, the disappearance of Colber, and the decline of Radipole.

Its impact should not be underestimated with a third to a half of the population killed, but it was for many the final blow that served to accelerate a decline which had its origins generations earlier. Its endemic nature meant that the disease continued to affect the population for centuries thereafter. The outbreaks of plague in 1361 and 1381, for example, were as equally serious as that of 1348.

There are no statistics giving precise numbers of people who died as a result of the Black Death. The scale of the disaster can only be inferred from records such as the institutions of clergy. At Winterborne Clenston four successive rectors were appointed to the living in 1348-9, at Winterborne Houghton there were three, and in many other parishes new priests followed one another in quick succession. The priest working within the community was at greatest risk - an occupational hazard. One hundred new institutions were made during the seven months from October 1348 to April 1349. The crisis led the Bishop of Bath and Wells to relax the normal rules and he issued instructions that: 'The Sacrament of the Eucharist, when no priest is available, may be adminstered by a deacon. If, however, there is no priest to administer the Sacrament of Extreme Unction, then, as in other matters, faith must suffice'.

In July 1349 the accounts of the estates held by the Crown around Bere Regis and Charminster reported no income was received because, 'the mortality of men in the present pestilence is so great that the lands thereof be untilled and the profits are lost'.

The smaller villages and hamlets which were already ailing, or those established on poorer land, would have felt the effects first. As labour became scarcer and tenancies fell vacant, holdings were amalgamated, and peasants moved away. Landowners, including the great monastic landlords, unable to attract tenants to work their arable land turned it over to sheep grazing. From the fourteenth century the enclosure of arable land for pasture became a feature of the rural landscape, particularly on the chalk downlands. To maintain rents, with a reduced labour market, many landlords found it was more profitable to turn to sheep.

Within the local settlement hierarchy, the less important places, dependent upon larger and more stable settlements, were deserted first. Villages which survived did not escape altogether and many show signs of shrinkage with tell-tale earthworks suggesting that the village was formerly much larger.

ISOLATED CHURCHES, EARTHWORKS AND OTHER CLUES

Isolated parish churches and earthworks are the most obvious indicators of former settlements. Other clues to look for in the landscape include the apparently random junction of footpaths and trackways in the middle of nowhere; the abrupt end to a road; gaps on maps with areas devoid of houses; the shape of the parish boundary; and the field pattern of walls, hedges and ditches.

Churches, now standing at some distance from the present village or with only the manor house as close neighbour, have always been appreciated as a beacon of settlement change, and Dorset has a number of note - Winterborne Came, Toller Fratrum, Winterborne Clenston, Up Cerne, Stockwood, Batcombe, Melbury Bubb and Nether Cerne to name a few. The church at the centre of its ecclesiastical parish had a vested interest, both spiritual and financial, in the health of the community which it served. As the religious focus it is often the oldest surviving building in the parish. Outward appearances may be deceptive, the result of enthusiastic Victorian renovation and rebuilding, but the font within will often confirm the church's medieval origins, while a number retain fragments of Anglo-Saxon sculpture or architectural detail, as at Winterbourne Steepleton and West Stour.

Any list of isolated churches would have to include Winterborne Tomson (now in the parish of Anderson). The church is a rare survival of an aisleless twelfth-century building, now in the care of the Churches Conservation Trust. It stands adjacent to a large farmstead, within confusing earthworks which may in part be the remains of the formal early seventeenth-century garden landscaping attached to the manor house. The village was never large, and the lack of references in later tax assessments would suggest a population of less than ten by 1428.

The isolated position of a church, such as the early medieval church of St
Andrew at Winterborne Tomson, is often the first clue to suggest the
existence of a former village.

The hill-top location of Silton church affords a vantage point from
which to gaze across the neighbouring field towards Judge Wyndham's
oak, which was once at the centre of the now long-deserted village.

Stock Gaylard, now in Lydlinch, was formerly a separate parish, of
which only the church remains close by Stock Gaylard House, an
eighteenth-century mansion set within an immense deer-park, well-
stocked with fallow deer. At Domesday the village had a population of
eleven. The church was not taxed in 1291 and by 1304 only two
people were listed as belonging to the manor. The last documentary
record is of 1333 when only three villagers were listed in the Subsidy
Rolls.

An even greater testimony to decline are the church ruins at
Knowlton, Winterborne Farringdon, Burleston and Stanton St
Gabriel. Knowlton (Woodlands) is of particular interest because of the

pagan and Christian use of a single site, the ruined church standing as it does within the encircling earthworks of a prehistoric henge *(see frontispiece and page 4 for photographs)*. The chancel and nave are of twelfth-century date and the church was still in use in 1550. But attendance declined and in 1659 the churchwardens tried to demolish it. They were refused permission and despite a short revival in its fortunes, the roof fell in and the church was abandoned in the eighteenth century. The remains of the village lie to the north-west on the banks of the River Allen, a close neighbour to the former settlement of Brockington (Gussage All Saints). The earthworks of both are damaged but show a number of closes and house sites.

The early failure of some communities is documented by the amalgamation of parishes which record the virtual desertion of a handful of villages by the mid-fifteenth century. Frome Belet or Billet, for example, was united with West Stafford by 1470. The name is derived from William Belet who held the manor at Domesday. The well-preserved earthworks of the village survive to the west of Stafford House. In 1332 eleven households were listed in the Lay Subsidy, paying a total of 28s 9d. The lord at the time was William de Euerard, liable to the highest contribution of 8s. When presented with a list of names it is idle but interesting to wonder just how well neighbours got on with one another, who was related to whom, and if your name was 'Swynhurde' how many pigs did you look after. To complete the tally for Frome Billet, in 1332 taxes were demanded as follows: 'de Johanne Mosse 2s, de Johanne atte Mede 2s, de Rogero Swynhurde 2s 9d, de Rogero Mosse 2s, de Johanne Edward 12d, de Thoma Bronyng 2s, de Johanne Osbern 12d, de Waltero atte Mede 2s, de Johanne Gym 2s, de Priore Dorcestr 4s.'.

The parish of Lazerton was united with Stourpaine in 1431 because 'the church of Lazerton had so small profits that it had been and was then destitute of a chaplain'. The village population had always been small, with less than thirty inhabitants at Domesday. In the late twelfth century the parish was so poor that it was released 'from all payments except synodals'. A decline to less than ten meant it was not taxed in 1428. The place-name is derived from the Old English meaning 'farm of the leech gatherers'. The village earthworks were destroyed in 1962 when levelling in Bones (Boons) Field, on the site of St Andrew's

Hutchins described the church at Wytherstone as 'ruinated long since'.
A stone carving of a hare playing a harp, now in Dorset County Museum,
is said to have come from the site of the church. The village is represented
today by a complex of farm buildings and houses.

Church, uncovered a fragment of a limestone coffin lid decorated with
an incised cross.

Hutchins is a prime source for former chapelries or 'fallen church
buildings', often a useful pointer to former chapels of ease or churches
which have since been combined with neighbouring parishes. At
Frome Whitfield (now in Stinsford) the churchwardens in 1606
reported that 'Mr Henry James our parson is not resident with us and
hath been absent about six years, and there hath been no service in
that time. The church is filled up with hay and corne and is so far in
decay that it is like to fall down'. By 1610 depopulation was complete
and the parish was united with Holy Trinity, Dorchester. Hutchins
recorded the parish had 'been of long time utterly dispeopled and was
then without church or chapel'. The remains of the village lie in the
vicinity of Frome Whitfield House, disturbed by later water meadows
and garden landscaping.

The church at Wytherstone (Powerstock) belonged to Abbotsbury
Abbey at the Dissolution but it was already in decay by the early
1500's. Hutchins wrote that the village was depopulated and the
church 'ruinated long since'. Other examples which he lists include

East Chelborough church, which though built no earlier than the sixteenth century, and added to in the eighteenth, stands on the site of a twelfth century predecessor.

West Woodyates (now in Pentridge), Woolcombe Matravers (now in Melbury Bubb), Buckland Ripers (now in Chickerell), Belchalwell (now in Okeford Fitzpaine), Ailwell (now in Frome St Quentin), Overcombe (now in Castleton), and Littleton (in Blandford St Mary).

But a word of caution: in an area of dispersed settlement, an isolated church would not be unusual, serving as it does a parish composed of scattered hamlets and farmsteads, and lacking a village focus.

Local folklore, myth and legend cannot be ignored and can be called upon to explain the mysterious disappearance of some villages. Fairies, according to tradition, were responsible for the isolated site of the church of East Chelborough which stands in a secluded spot at Lewcombe, one mile to the north. The villagers made three attempts to build a church, but each time fairies who lived on Castle Hill carried the foundation stones to Lewcombe.

More reliable than local legends are the humps and bumps indicating the site of a deserted village. The houses and small gardens that formed the core of the village were often enclosed by a boundary bank or back lane to separate the inhabited area from the surrounding fields. Roadways leading into the village often survive as sunken features or hollow-ways, eroded over centuries by the passage of animals and carts, as in the deep lanes in the west of the county.

Information gleaned from field survey and archaeological excavation by the archaeologists on television's *Time Team* has been combined to enable Victor Ambrus to reconstruct a single medieval longhouse standing in its croft. What survive as humps and bumps in a pasture field are shown to be the walls and foundations of a small homestead.

In stony areas, raised mounds or platforms indicate former house sites (tofts) and will appear as square or rectangular features. By their nature, if undisturbed by later ploughing, they survive with a crisper definition compared with houses whose walls were built of turf, timber or cob which, when abandoned, leave a flatter, wider spread of material.

The toft was the medieval equivalent of a farmyard, with house, outbuildings, barns, and byres providing shelter for both humans and animals. Ancillary buildings might include a granary, henhouse, pigsty, stable, sheepcote, oxhouse or carthouse. People and animals usually occupied separate buildings but the longhouse, still familiar in Dorset and Devon today, accommodated both humans and animals under one roof. It was divided in two by a cross-passage, between opposing doorways often set in the middle of the long walls. One end, with a central hearth for cooking and heating, provided the living accommodation for the family. The byre at the other end sheltered the animals, or was used as a store for farm produce and equipment.

Attached to each toft, the croft was an area of land used as a garden or orchard, or as a paddock for animals, depending on its size. Some crofts were large enough to be ploughed: it has been suggested that at

Holworth ramps in the north-west corner of each croft may have allowed an ox team access to the surrounding common fields.

But, to avoid disappointment, it has to be said that the vast majority of sites, unlike Bardolfeston, do not have such spectacular earthworks. For many there is no coherent plan, and earthworks, if they survive, can be vague and formless. And there are the enigmatic puzzles, such as the prominent but nameless site to the west of Weatherby Castle. The scarps and banks of a rectangular enclosure with internal divisions and possible house platforms lie on the west side of the Milborne Brook, to the south of Milborne St Andrew. The settlement pattern within the parish is very complicated and assigning a name to the village, if that is what it is, is problematic. The course of the stream has been canalised in part and later landscaping has disturbed the site.

The string of small settlements to the east of Portesham, at Waddon, Little Waddon, and Corton, made full use of the available land. Victor Ambrus, for *Time Team*, has reconstructed the crofts with their longhouses and surrounding fields running down into the valley, while the hills above provided grazing for sheep.

The earthworks of an anonymous site, south of Milborne St Andrew, survive as a rectangular enclosure of two acres, with a number of closes bisected by modern farm tracks (looking south).

Professor Good reports 'a remarkable local tradition, long held in the neighbouring village, that a golden coffin is buried in the Culeaze and that attempts to find it bring on storms of thunder and lightning. This, surely, must be a folk-memory of the ancient village.'

The planned linear character of several villages can be seen in the regular arrangement of tofts and crofts which survive as earthworks at Holworth, West Ringstead, East Hemsworth, West Woodsford and Friar Mayne. At Rew, in Winterborne St Martin (Martinstown), a row of nine roughly rectangular crofts survive on a steep slope above the river in a field called Hanging Meadow. The name Rew (row; as of houses or trees) is first documented in the thirteenth century and aptly describes the character of the site. Although long since abandoned the field was part of Townfield Farm on an estate map of 1768, a place-name indicating former habitation but not a 'town' as such.

Settlement is surprisingly mobile, and is not as static within the landscape as might be supposed. As well as disappearing completely, settlements can contract, shift and mutate, changing form and extent over time.

The visible surviving earthworks represent only the last phase of the village's development on the eve of desertion, and may conceal earlier structures and alignments, often of a quite complex character and which in themselves will be a record of expansion and contraction during the settlement's life. Houses could be rebuilt on several different alignments without altering the basic boundary arrangement which, as a property demarcation, would have been jealously guarded.

Shrunken or contracted villages are much more common than deserted sites but the earthwork remains are the same, surviving in grassy paddocks in gaps along the street frontage. Such earthworks are at most risk now as prime sites for building development and infilling. Earthworks as evidence for contraction or shift can be seen at Coombe Keynes, Long Crichel, Chilcombe and in a string of settlements along the South Winterborne valley near Charminster. A map of Hilton surveyed by William Woodward shows a number of paddocks or closes along the road to the south-west of the village which were still in use in 1771 although the house sites themselves had been abandoned.

Fire has always been a major hazard affecting not only towns, such as Blandford and Wareham, but having equally devastating consequences in villages. In 1542 John Leland in visiting Horton reported the village had recently suffered a fire, 'the village was now a late brent'; while gaps in the street frontage of Sixpenny Handley have a more recent origin as the result of a fire in 1892 which started in a wheelwright's shop leaving one hundred homeless.

ABANDONMENT

The later fourteenth and fifteenth centuries in Dorset are noted for the villages, such as Holworth, West Ringstead and Friar Mayne, which were either abandoned or reduced to a hamlet or single farm.

Holworth now occupies an odd westerly extrusion of Chaldon Herring parish. It was formerly a detached part of Milton Abbas parish, a block of land granted to Milton Abbey by King Athelstan in 933. A complex of scarps and banks cover an area of 6 acres to the

Holworth is one of the few deserted villages to have been excavated. The former village street survives as a sunken way running east-west, bordered to the north by a single row of houses with gardens and fields running down the slope towards the stream.

Glebe Cottage, in the trees at the bottom of the picture, occupies the site of the former church of West Ringstead. The hollow-way marks the line of the village street as it drops southwards towards the sea (at top).

east of Holworth Farm, and represent the former street, house sites and gardens of a planned, single-row village. A string of seven enclosures (tofts) line the north side of the street, with long narrow fields (crofts) beyond, defined by banks or low scarps.

In 1936 trial excavations recovered fragments of thirteenth-century medieval pottery. Further excavations in 1958 established two periods of occupation. The first, ante-dating the toft layout, was represented by a number of pits, ditches and a few post-holes containing pottery of the twelfth to thirteenth century or earlier. The second period was marked by the stone footings of a structure with its long axis parallel to the street. This may have been a three-roomed house, or two buildings separated by a yard. The footings would have supported a timber framework and there was evidence to suggest at least two phases of rebuilding. There was no archaeological evidence for settlement after the fifteenth century, and indeed the last documentary reference for Holworth is in the Lay Subsidy Roll of 1333 when fourteen persons were listed.

West Ringstead (in Osmington), unlike Holworth, was once a separate parish with its own church. Domesday Book describes four Ringsteads: West, Middle, East and Upringstede, each of which appears to have been a separate settlement with a total recorded population of nineteen. The Lay Subsidy Roll of 1327 lists seventeen people within the parish. Continuing population decline is shown when in 1428 the parish was taxed for one mark only, an indication that there were at least ten inhabitants (but probably only just). Villagers struggled to make a living, and a Court Roll of 1447 called for reparations to be made to the 'hall and grange' of John Styvens, and to the 'hall and grange' of William Drake and other buildings. A note of discord was reported in 1463 when John Wynkeley attacked John Kymer with a scythe. In 1488 poverty resulted in the rectory of Ringstead being united with the vicarage of Osmington.

The earthworks of West Ringstead deserted village cover an area of ten acres on the coast at Ringstead Bay, two miles south-west of Holworth. They are fairly well preserved, but a system of sluices and channels constructed as part of a water-meadow system have disturbed the area to the south-west of Glebe Cottage.

The village street drops southwards as a hollow-way towards the coast, with the sites of at least eight houses grouped at the northern end, to the south of Glebe Cottage. The cottage itself incorporates the thirteenth-century chancel and chancel arch of the former parish church, first referred to in documents in 1227. The church appears to have been largely destroyed or abandoned when the village was deserted in late medieval times. Local tradition describes how the

Earthworks and a hollow-way to the north of Little Mayne Farm (centre) mark the site of one of the four settlements which once existed in the parish of West Knighton.

French landed and sacked the village, burning down the church while the priest stood at the altar.

The outline of the medieval parish of West Knighton enclosed four distinct settlements, each with their associated open fields. West Knighton lies at the centre with the parish church of St Peter. To the north, the medieval settlement of Lewell or East Stafford is now represented by Lower Lewell Farm and Lewell Mill. Little Mayne, the third settlement, is now reduced to a single farm in the south-west of the parish, with slight earthworks and a hollow-way. Hutchins records a free chapel of St Stephen, whose last recorded rector was instituted in 1491.

To the south-east, the former village of Friar Mayne survived as relatively well-preserved earthworks until their destruction in 1963. A well-defined hollow-way ran west to east, bordered by house sites which ranged in size from 12 x 20ft to 35 x 90ft. Ploughing has severely damaged the site, revealing the walls to have been of cob. The closes running back from the house sites were bounded by banks or scarps, enclosing up to a quarter of an acre of ground in some cases. The site of a chapel, described as 'slighted' in 1650, lay close to Fryer Mayne house.

The earthwork remains of the former hamlet of East Hemsworth (in Witchampton) lie to the north of Hemsworth Farm. They have been disturbed by quarrying and a modern track, but a broad hollow-way running SE to NW is bounded on the east by 7-8 closes containing the disturbed remains of houses. East Hemsworth, together with the neighbouring settlement of West Hemsworth, each recorded a population of four at Domesday, and each was taxed at one hide. Subsequent references are lacking, and by 1770 when Isaac Taylor

Two Hemsworths were recorded in Domesday Book. Today the site of the deserted hamlet of East Hemsworth survives to the north of Hemsworth Farm, with a number of closes bisected by the modern farm road and disturbed by quarrying.

drew the estate map the site of East Hemsworth was called Cow Lease.

Witchampton is of interest in itself as an example of a shrunken village. In addition there is evidence to suggest that the site continued to be occupied from Roman times at least until the Saxon conquest. Prior to ploughing, earthworks in Bushy Park Field comprised a double row of house sites on both sides of Frog Lane, running north from the village. Fieldwalking picked up a selection of pottery, including Roman and post-medieval sherds. The majority of the sherds were twelfth and thirteenth century, with some even earlier pieces. Together they would suggest that the area was occupied from the time of the Norman conquest until the fourteenth century.

The four parishes of the Upper Winterborne valley now comprise Winterborne Houghton, Winterborne Stickland, Winterborne Clenston and Winterborne Whitechurch; with settlements today focussed on the villages of Houghton, Stickland and Whitechurch and the hamlet of Whatcombe in Whitechurch.

The medieval settlement pattern was far more complex, and missing from the valley are the villages of Quarleston in Stickland parish; Philipston, Nicholson and Clenston in Clenston parish; and La Lee in Whitechurch. All have been either abandoned or reduced to a single farmstead. In many cases the village earthworks which survived up to the 1960s have been destroyed since, but aerial photographs and maps can help to reconstruct the earlier boundaries for each estate or tithing.

The regularity of many of the earthworks suggests a planned and ordered layout of closes within each village. To the west of Winterborne Stickland, seventeen survive as slight earthworks, ranging in width from 45ft to 90ft, on the south side of the stream, with an almost mirror image of closes to the north. The tithing of Quarleston with its associated village lay at the extreme southern end of the parish of Stickland. Six parallel closes, 240ft long and 84ft to 90ft wide, survived until the 1950s to the east of the stream. Pottery collected from the field dates from the eleventh to thirteenth centuries.

Clenston in medieval times was divided into the three tithings of Philipston, Clenston, and Nicholson. The parish church of St Nicholas survives in the former tithing of Nicholson. Many of the earthworks

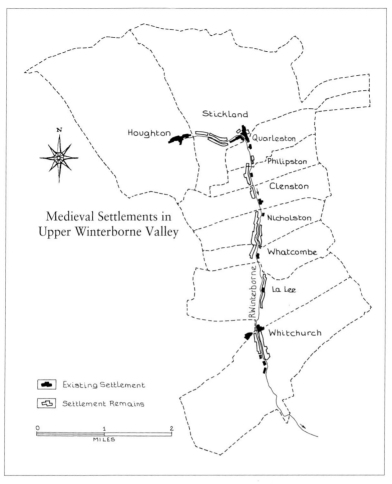

Medieval Settlements in
Upper Winterborne Valley

Existing Settlement

Settlement Remains

Earthworks and estate boundaries record a string of deserted settlements along the Upper Winterborne valley. All the clues are present: an isolated church, single farms, earthworks (both upstanding and ploughed-out), and long field boundaries running from the river up the valley sides.

have now been destroyed but a survey of Philipston by the Royal Commission and aerial photographs again record the planned regularity of each settlement.

The tithing of Whatcombe in Winterborne Whitechurch is now represented by the farmsteads at Higher Whatcombe and, until their destruction in 1966, six rectangular closes survived on the west of the stream, with others to the east. To the south the tithing of La Lee was held by Milton Abbey at the time of the Domesday survey. The emparking and landscaping associated with Whatcombe House has disturbed the site of the former village.

Between the present village of Winterborne Whitechurch and the hamlet of Lower Street, twenty-seven long rectangular closes were recorded by the Royal Commission on both sides of the stream.

The consistency of width, on a multiple of 30ft, is a remarkable indicator of the planned character and regular layout of the string of settlements along the valley. Without excavation it is impossible to give a precise date, but this expansion of population must have taken place between 1086 and 1300. The numerous entries for 'Winterborne' in Domesday Book makes it difficult to associate documentary references with individual villages. Winterborne La Lee, held by Milton Abbey, is perhaps the exception. Now represented by the farm and estate buildings of Lower Whatcombe, in 1086 the land was worked by two bordars and one slave.

The decline in population after 1300 is suggested by assessing the number of taxpayers listed in the Subsidy Roll of 1332 against the number of closes surviving as earthworks along the valley bottom. Christopher Taylor has calculated that even allowing for tax evasion, there are too few people listed to occupy them all. At Winterborne Whitechurch, for example, there were twenty-four taxpayers in 1332 occupying 27 closes, and twelve taxpayers at Clenston, Philipston and Nicholson would have been hard pressed to fill the minimum of 31 closes surviving there as earthworks.

Within the wider landscape, deserted hamlets and farmsteads also bear testimony to the decline in population and the change in agricultural practices.

West Burton, in Winfrith Newburgh, is just one of a number of small settlements, or hamlets, sited along the edge of the heathland, stretching from East Burton through West Burton and East Knighton to East Fossil. It was a flourishing hamlet until at least the early fourteenth century, before declining by the mid sixteenth century. The surviving earthworks cover ten acres and consist of hollow-ways meeting at a T-junction with at least ten rectangular closes. Pottery

The deserted medieval hamlet of Modbury has long been recorded on
Ordnance Survey maps. From the air the modern road can be seen to bisect
the settlement earthworks which lie in pasture above the stream (north is
towards bottom right).

picked up from the fields dates from the twelfth to fourteenth
centuries.

The deserted hamlet of Modbury (Swyre) is now bisected by a
minor road between Berwick and Bredy, and survives as a group of
disturbed low-lying banks and ditches in pasture. The site has never
truly been lost, its name surviving on a series of maps, including the
1839 Tithe Map and the 25-inch Ordnance Survey of 1891 which
plots 'Modbury (site of)' in wonderful Gothic script. Pottery from the
site would suggest depopulation in the fifteenth century, with a
corresponding change from arable to pasture. Hutchins wrote that the
site was 'in ruins and depopulated beyond the memory of man'.

On a smaller scale but of equal interest is the enclosed hamlet
discovered at Buckler's Bottom, straddling the boundary between the
parishes of West Compton and Compton Valence (see following page
for photograph). The well-preserved remains are of an unnamed
settlement which was probably deserted in the fourteenth century. The
site is very similar to another, now destroyed by ploughing, in
Compton Valence parish, 500 yards to the south-east.

Many more deserted minor settlements such as these remain to be
located where scattered hamlets and farmsteads were common. Lost

The small hamlet at Buckler's Bottom straddles the parish boundary between Compton Valence (to left) and West Compton. A hollow-way crosses the valley bottom from left to right, while the spring provided a necessary water source for the cluster of houses (north is to bottom right).

villages may be more dramatic, but their smaller neighbours were equally vulnerable. Recent aerial photography has picked up a previously unrecorded area of earthworks at Higher Attisham (Broadwindsor). The place-name 'Hadesham' is first recorded in 1244, meaning the 'enclosure belonging to a man called Aeddi'.

Shrinkage and desertion of settlements was accompanied by the large-scale reduction in arable cultivation and the conversion to pasture. Many of the arable fields created in the twelfth and thirteenth centuries, particularly those on the higher downland slopes, reverted to grassland.

In the valley bottoms, common fields belonging to deserted settlements were enclosed in the late medieval period. Precise dating is difficult. However, at Ranston, in the Iwerne valley, the common fields which had formerly occupied a large area of the parish in 1274, had disappeared completely by the late fifteenth century. Similarly, at

Winterborne Clenston, enclosure of the three-field system was effective and the village was deserted by the mid fifteenth century.

The decline in the acreage of arable land was matched by an increase in the size of sheep flocks on the newly converted pastures. With fewer human mouths to feed, and the increased wealth to be gained by the export of wool and cloth, the need to run arable and sheep as a combined agricultural system was less pressing. The profits to be gained led to a dramatic increase in flock sizes. By 1330 over 1000 sheep were folded at Buckland Newton, one of the estates of Glastonbury Abbey, while Bindon Abbey in 1329-30 had over 7000 sheep on its manors.

In 1435 and 1449, 137 villages and hamlets, scattered over the county, asked for and received a reduction in taxation on account of poverty. For others, able to take advantage of the difficulties of neighbours, this was a period of prosperity. The new wealth gained from wool was channelled into enlarging and embellishing parish churches, and the building of new manor houses.

The fourteenth and fifteenth centuries saw the rise of new gentry families such as the Martyns of Athelhampton, and the Latimer family

Aerial photographs, such as this of Higher Attisham, reveal tantalising cropmarks which point to the site of a probable medieval settlement. The place-name is often significant – in this case, the 'enclosure belonging to a man called Aeddi'.

Low sun highlights the banks and scarps of hollow-ways and house platforms surviving in unploughed parkland to the south of St Andrew's church at Bingham's Melcombe. One of two deserted villages in the parish, the Bingham's acquired the manor in the thirteenth century, while their neighbours, the Horsey's at Melcombe Horsey, were relatively late arrivals in the reign of Henry VII.

of Duntish manor. The Binghams had lived at Bingham's Melcombe since the thirteenth century, increasing their wealth by trade and astute estate management. They were responsible for rebuilding the church in the mid fourteenth century and their own manor house. The former village survives as a sequence of embanked enclosures either side of an east-west hollow-way to the south of the parish church.

At neighbouring Melcombe Horsey or Higher Melcombe, the Horsey family acquired the manor by marriage in the reign of Henry VII. The site of the now deserted village lies in 'Chapel Close' to the north-west of the former manor house, and, although damaged by quarrying, the outlines of several rectangular closes and house sites are discernible. Throughout their history, the records for Bingham's Melcombe and Melcombe Horsey have been interlinked, making it difficult to disentangle the two manors, but depopulation of both appears to have been complete by the early fifteenth century.

PROFIT IN PASTURE

The Dissolution of the Monasteries in 1539 and the break-up of their estates led to a major redistribution of property. The sixteenth and seventeenth centuries were a period of great social and economic change and increased prosperity. Yeoman farmers who had formerly leased the land they worked were now able to buy. Farming became increasingly specialised, trade and commerce expanded. The new secular landlords enjoyed a new social status and enhanced their estates and homes accordingly.

A survey of leading Dorset families in 1634 shows that nearly half of them appeared for the first time between 1529 and 1603: amongst them the Tregonwells at Milton Abbey, the Strangways at Melbury Sampford, the Strode family at Parnham, Sir John Digby at Sherborne, and Sir John Banks at Corfe Castle.

In 1540 John Leland wrote of Melbury House at Melbury Sampford, 'Mr Strangeguayse hath now a late much buildid at Mylbyri quadrato, avauncing the inner part of the house with a loftie and fresch tower'. The family, originally from Yorkshire, profited from the Dissolution and as one of the Commissioners Giles Strangways was able to acquire large monastic estates, both around Melbury and in the Blackmore Vale. Extensive landscaping of the deer park has obliterated all trace of the village, which presumably was close to the church.

Large-scale sheep farming was extremely profitable in the sixteenth and seventeenth centuries, and the decline of arable at the expense of pasture provided the final blow for many villages. The slow decline of many settlements continued, leading to their gradual desertion or reduction to a single farmstead.

Precise accuracy is difficult to gauge, but all contemporary writers report large flocks. Leland in 1540 wrote 'al about great flokkes of shepe'; Thomas Gerard in 1620 described the downs 'all overspread with innumerable Flockes of Sheepe for which it yields very good and sound Feeding, and from which the Countrie hath reapted an unknown Gaine'; and Edward Leigh in 1659 judged that there were 'within six miles of Dorchester three hundred thousand sheep'.

The poet and vicar of Bere Regis, Thomas Bastard, was born at Blandford Forum in 1566. Before his death in Dorchester Gaol in 1618 he succinctly summed up the situation:

Sheepe have eate up our meadows and our downes
Our corne, our wood, whole villages and towns

Large tracts of former open-fields and commons were enclosed to accommodate the expanding flocks. The common fields of Charminster were enclosed in 1577. At Iwerne Courtney (Shroton) a survey in 1548 reported: 'The Customary tenants were so smale and so little lande longing to them that they were not able to pay the Lords' rent, but one half of them departed the towne'. The land was enclosed and allocated amongst the remaining four tenants.

Not all enclosure went smoothly and many tenants questioned the actions of their landlords. At Stour Provost in 1620 tenants of Kings College, Cambridge, objected to the re-allocation of the arable land, but were finally forced to agree 'albeit after much solicitation and entreaty'. Sir Anthony Ashley of Wimborne St Giles threatened to increase the size of his own flock and extend his rabbit warren if his tenants disagreed with his plans in 1604. The tenants of Winterborne Steepleton and Fordington held out until 1861 and 1876 respectively when enclosure was enforced by Act of Parliament; while parts of Portland are still worked on an open-field regime.

Enclosure of large areas of former open downland continued with Long Bredy enclosed in 1597; Hooke, North Poorton, and Toller Porcorum in 1620; Bradford Peverell in 1741; and Blackdown Hill in Broadwindsor in 1677. At Puddletown in 1629 the old common meadows were enclosed to create the innovative water meadows, which were to extend along many of the chalk streams of the county.

Early enclosures usually produced fields which were small and irregular in shape. The field boundaries are often sinuous, and follow the line of the arable strips of the open-field system. The enclosures created by Act of Parliament in the period 1750 to 1850 are typically large and rectangular, when extensive tracts of the village fields were taken as a whole and reallocated in compact parcels of land, with farmhouses and barns built in the middle of the new holdings.

For the evicted tenants the effects of enclosure were dire, especially in a county which had little to offer in way of alternative employment. The drift to developing industrial towns and cities as in the North and Midlands was not an option. Enclosure often meant the loss of rights to commons, and the means to supplement diet and income by keeping a cow or a couple of sheep.

William Holloway in his poem *The Peasant's Fate* (1802) railed against the enclosure of the commons and the expulsion of the labourers and small farmers.

Now into one a hundred fields are thrown,
Their tenants banish'd, and their pleasures flown!

And half depopulate their native land! ...

Where now the park extends, and useless deer
Along the solitary glades appear,
Rich corn fields wav'd, in spacious prospect spread,
Nor felt one villager the want of bread.

Holloway was born in 1761 at Whatcombe, the younger son of a small yeoman farmer, while his grandparents had lived at neighbouring La Lee. Both hamlets, within Winterborne Whitechurch, preserve evidence of depopulation, no doubt providing Holloway with first-hand experience of the dramatic changes in the countryside around his home.

There are few instances where a precise date can be given to date the moment of desertion. Mapperton is perhaps the exception, and unique if the tale is true. Visitors today can enjoy and appreciate the idyllic setting of manor house, stable block and church at the head of a landscaped valley. In 1666 the parish was devastated by plague. The churchyard was not consecrated and parishioners carried their dead for burial in neighbouring Netherbury. Fearful of the infection spreading, the people of Netherbury refused burial to the dead of Mapperton, and the coffins were left on the parish boundary, at a spot now marked by the Posy or Cosy Tree. A small enclosure on the top

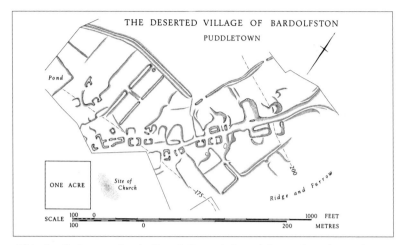

THE DESERTED VILLAGE OF BARDOLFSTON
PUDDLETOWN

Pond

ONE ACRE

Site of
Church

Ridge and Furrow

SCALE

FEET
METRES

This detailed survey by the Royal Commission of the earthwork remains at
Bardolfeston helps to clarify the last phase of the village layout before it
was finally abandoned. The rectangular outlines of longhouses border the
village street, with their doorways still clearly recognisable.

of South Warren Hill is said to mark the plague pit dug for all those
who died in 1666.

More often the slow decline over generations is signalled by the
realisation that the settlement is no longer listed in any of the major
tax assessments, as in the case of Bardolfeston, Whitcombe,
Winterborne Farringdon and Winterborne Came.

Bardolfeston (Puddletown), as stated earlier, is a truly remarkable
survival and one of the best sites in Dorset to visit, made accessible by
the landowner under the Countryside Stewardship Scheme. It lies on
the north side of the River Piddle, to the north-west of Athelhampton
House. Approaching from the south, the seventeenth-century water
meadows are a prominent feature with their geometric maze of
channels and leats. The medieval village site itself is under pasture and
sits slightly above the floodplain.

Originally a parish in its own right, held by the Prior of
Christchurch Twynham, the probable site of the church is indicated by
the field-name Church Knap. In the early fourteenth century only
seven taxpayers were recorded, perhaps indicating that the village was
already in decline. The few remaining residents in 1512 paid a subsidy

Bardolfeston is one of the best-preserved deserted medieval village sites in the county. Modern farm tracks cut across the former village street which runs left to right (north towards top right).

of 18s 4d, but the absence of any reference in the Hearth Tax returns would suggest it was deserted by the seventeenth century.

The village extends over 15 acres, with well-preserved earthworks, destroyed in part by the water meadows to the south, and quarrying at the northern end of the village street. Within its lifetime, the village underwent large-scale alteration, and at least two changes in plan and layout are visible in the pattern of earthworks. The earliest phase of the village is represented by a roughly L-shaped area of rectangular closes bounded by banks and scarps. On top, and at a slight angle, sits the later phase, with a broad hollow-way running SW-NE across the site, flanked by house sites. These comprise rectangular areas varying in size from 20 x 12ft to 40 x 18ft, bounded by banks or walls of flint rubble, up to 2ft high. The earthworks are some of the best in the

The church at Whitcombe stands isolated, surrounded by earthworks, and with its close neighbours at Winterborne Came and Winterborne Farringdon may well have provided the inspiration for William Barnes' poem, *The Depopulated Village.*

county. Most houses show clearly as longhouses with opposed entrances, lying parallel to the street frontage, with in some instances subsidiary outbuildings in the closes to the rear.

The compact hamlet of Whitcombe, east of Dorchester, now comprises a group of thatched eighteenth-century cottages with a manor house and seventeenth-century barn set around a small green. The church stands in splendid solitude encircled by an eighteenth-century brick wall. Earthworks in fields to the east and north-east show the former extent of the village. The manor was granted by Athelstan to Milton Abbey, and at the Dissolution passed to the Tregonwells.

The church contains fragments of two tenth-century stone crosses, decorated with interlace pattern; and magnificent wall paintings of the fifteenth century, one of which depicts St Christopher carrying Christ. As rector of Winterborne Came, the poet William Barnes had close associations with the church and took his first and last services here.

The table-tomb by the porch records the death of the wonderfully-named Melchisedeck Gillet, aged 75, in September 1680. Although we know little about him, it is just possible that he was one of the wealthier farmers who took the opportunity to extend their grazing rights and thus increase the size of their sheep flocks at the expense of the former tenants.

The rector of Winterborne Came, Joseph Bateman, was certainly in dispute with him in 1680 over tithes payable on land at Winterborne Came and Farringdon, a case which went to the Court of Exchequer. In addition to owning land at Watercombe, Gillet also leased extensive pastures in Fordington, West Knighton, West Stafford, Cripton, Winterborne Came and Farringdon. His flock of over 2,200 sheep were constantly on the move between the scattered grazing fields, frustrating Joseph Bateman's attempts to levy tithes on the sheep because of their endless perambulations.

Winterborne Farringdon is but one of a string of deserted sites along the south Winterborne valley. Writing in 1620 Thomas Gerard described 'a lone church, for there is hardlie any house left in the Parish, such of late hath been the Covetousness of some private Men, that to increase their Demesnes have depopulated whole parishes'. By 1773 Hutchins wrote that Farringdon 'is entirely depopulated and has been so beyond the memory of man'. The Hearth Tax of 1662 has no entry for Winterborne Farringdon while its immediate neighbour Winterborne Came had only two households.

A complaint to the Court of Star Chamber in 1521 stated that the landlord of Winterborne Came, Sir William Fyloll, was enclosing the common pastures for his sheep, and his tenants were not able to pay their rent nor 'Able to Abide in theire countrey by cause of the said greate oppressions' of their landlord which included overstocking the commons, destruction of their crops with his sheep and cattle, and driving his carts and wains across their arable land.

The causes of depopulation are often cumulative, and there is evidence that both Farringdon and Came were experiencing decline as early as the fourteenth century. An 'improving' landlord would have no difficulty in finding sufficient reason to encourage the stragglers to leave, and thus earn the opprobrium of others.

Winterborne Farringdon, to the south of Dorchester, sits on higher ground above the water meadows of the South Winterborne (looking south). The upstanding east gable of the church, caught by the sunlight, sits at the centre of a network of enclosures and is approached by a deep hollow-way from the west.

Until the seventeenth century Winterborne Farringdon or Germayne was a separate parish. The east gable of St German's church still stands at the centre of the extensive remains of the deserted village. The ruins of the church were used by Thomas Hardy as the trysting place for John, the trumpet-major, and the heroine, Anne Garland, in his novel *The Trumpet Major*. 'Yes, this field used to be a village. My grandfather could call to mind when there were houses here. But the squire pulled 'em down, because poor folk were an eyesore to him.'

If it is difficult to give a precise date for the desertion of individual villages, it is equally daunting to assess the demise of single farms or hamlets. Shrunken hamlets have been identified at Notton and Cruxton in Maiden Newton, and at Lower Kingcombe in Toller

The ruins of the church of St German at Winterborne Farringdon photographed in 1905 – the 'lone church for there is hardlie anie house left in the parish', incorporating a fourteenth-century window and stones from a fifteenth-century archway.

Porcorum. Excavations in and around the deserted site at Woolcombe (Toller Porcorum) suggest that it was not a hamlet but a farm attached to a substantial house, predecessor to the present farmhouse. As a class of settlement the excavators describe it as 'a gentry residence and working farm with resident cottage tenants/estate employees'. The whole integrated complex was probably the work of Robert Bingham (approximately 1245-1303), and excavated material suggests the area was occupied between the twelfth and sixteenth centuries.

COUNTRY HOUSES

Professor Ronald Good provided an impressive list of twenty-six former villages now represented by country houses. Of these Milton Abbas, Bryanston, Charborough, Eastbury, East Lulworth, Iwerne Stepleton, Kingston Lacy, Kingston Russell, Kingston Maurward, Moor Crichel, Encombe, Smedmore, Stinsford, and Winterborne Came epitomise the pride and desire of their owners to create a private park, detached from tenants and villagers.

A few notable examples described in detail will illustrate the power of the landowner in the eighteenth and nineteenth centuries. In the case of Milton Abbas and East Lulworth, deliberate removal of existing houses to enlarge the park took place, in other instances it was a case of fortuitous extension following previous desertion.

Maurice Beresford remarked, 'In the narrow sense of a "lost" village we cannot claim Milton Abbas among our number since the Earl built a magnificent compensatory village half a mile away'. Equally, at the height of its prosperity, the settlement enjoyed the status and importance of a town, with its own market and fairs, and a population of 400-500 inhabitants in the early fourteenth century, and so by a strict definition falls outside the scope of this book. However, the story embodies all the essential elements of an eighteenth-century lord removing a blot on the landscape so that he could enjoy an open parkland vista designed by the greatest landscape gardener of the day.

The original settlement was one of a long string of villages along the Milborne Brook and owed its prosperity and growth to the Benedictine abbey, founded by King Athelstan in the tenth century. The chancel, tower and transepts of the present church are all that survive of the fourteenth-century monastic church which replaced an earlier one destroyed by fire in 1309.

Set in a rich agricultural area, the dissolution of the monastery in

The estate map of Milton Abbas drawn by William Woodward in 1769-
1771 records accurately the extent of the former 'village' at Milton Abbas
before the site was cleared and its inhabitants removed to a model village
out of sight of Joseph Damer.

1539 had little effect on the town, which continued to prosper until 1771 when Joseph Damer (later Lord Milton, 1st Earl of Dorchester) evicted all the townsfolk to present 'Capability' Brown with a broad canvas on which to landscape the grounds around his new house.

The streets and individual house sites survive to the south-east of the house, but the former market place and High Street now lie buried beneath three feet of earth. The earthwork remains complement the plan of the town surveyed by William Woodward in 1769-1771, which traces the line of the High Street leading from Market Street into Newport Street, Broad Street and Duck Street.

Sir William Chambers, architect for the rebuilding of the house in 1771-76, described Joseph Damer as an 'unmannerly imperious lord'. Lord Milton's generosity in providing a new model village, set in a wooded side valley, was not achieved without a struggle. Woodward's plan records for each house plot the number of 'lives' left before Lord Milton could clear the village, and for nearly twenty years the view from the house must have resembled a demolition site, with a handful of entrenched householders determined to avoid eviction.

According to local tradition, Lord Milton's actions in removing the village and churchyard were because he was so incensed by the local boys stealing apples from his orchard. His gardeners refused to dig up the graves of their ancestors. In fury Lord Milton booted a skull into the corner of the field, shouting 'What! Are my men to be put off working by a lousy skull!' Retribution followed, Lord Milton fell ill and it was rumoured he was being eaten up by lice.

Although on a smaller scale, Humphrey Sturt's vision for Moor (More) Crichel followed the pattern of Joseph Damer at Milton Abbas. Hutchins records, 'There was once a commodious parsonage house in the parish but from it unfortunately standing in the way of the improvements of Mr Humphrey Sturt, soon after he came to the Napier estate he pulled it down and floated the whole site of it into a lake'.

The present manor house replaces an earlier one destroyed by fire in 1742. The Napier family who owned it started to rebuild but in 1765, following the failure of the male line, the estate passed to Humphrey Sturt of nearby Horton House. His advantageous marriage to Diana Napier allowed him to enlarge Crichel House and extend the

The site of the former village of Moor Crichel now lies submerged beneath the waters of the lake, the result of emparking by Humphrey Sturt in the late eighteenth century. The entire village was moved to what is now called New Town, leaving only the church (rebuilt in 1850) and a carefully contrived landscape in front of the classical mansion, which itself was largely rebuilt by Humphrey Sturt.

parkland with woods, copses and a large serpentine lake. The village street, flanked by rectangular closes, extended southwards from the church and manor house but by 1770 it had been demolished and the displaced villagers moved to New Town, in Witchampton parish, a mile away to the south. One house survives of this 'new village', with cob walls and thatched roof.

In medieval times Bryanston was a relatively large settlement, with 23 taxpayers recorded in 1333, but by 1662 the number of households had fallen to six and by the late eighteenth century only the manor house and church were marked on Isaac Taylor's map. Kip's engraving shows the early eighteenth-century manor house by the banks of the River Stour, set in an elaborate formal garden, with the parish church adjacent. In 1778 the house was demolished to be replaced by a new one designed by James Wyatt. This mansion in turn suffered the same fate as its predecessor when the present Bryanston House was built by Lord Portman in the 1890's in neo-classical style to designs by Norman Shaw. High on the downs, it is sited 500 yards to the north-west of the former village.

Taylor marks the site of Charborough (Morden) while Hutchins describes it as 'once a manor and hamlet, now extinguished and depopulated, consisting only of the seat of Mr Drax and a farmhouse. Foundations of houses have been dug up on the south side of the church, where the ancient vill probably stood'.

The village at Eastbury or Gunvil Eastbury (Tarrant Gunville) has had as chequered a career as that of its one-time owner, George Bubb Doddington (later Lord Melcombe). All but a fragment of Eastbury House, designed by Vanbrugh between 1718 and 1738, had been demolished by the end of the eighteenth century. The original village straddled the Tarrant stream and lay close to the present entrance gateway to the house.

John Leland in his *Itinerary* in 1546 wrote that 'the goodly maner place of the Newborows, Lords of East Lulleworth, is hard by the paroch-church'. All has since been transformed, and the one remaining fixed point of reference is the parish church of St Andrew at East Lulworth. The original manor house was demolished and replaced in 1608 by the idealised medieval castle that is now Lulworth Castle, recently restored following a disastrous fire in 1929. The original village survives as an area of low banks, platforms and hollows in parkland to the south-east of the church.

East Lulworth is fortunate, if not unique, in the survival of two representations of the village before emparking. A pictorial view of 1721 by Margaret Weld is a fascinating record of the village, full of life and activity, with ships out to sea, a haywain, horse-drawn wagons, and people strolling in the formal gardens of Lulworth Castle while deer graze in the surrounding park. The village houses with their neat gardens line the street leading to the church which stands just outside the park wall of the castle. The estate map, surveyed by J. Sparrow in 1770, shows houses along the village street, but all had been cleared by 1790, and the village of East Lulworth now lies half a mile to the east. The Welds offered to move the parish church if the parishioners paid for the tower, but they refused and a right of way had to be maintained across the park.

The Welds, a prominent Catholic family, as owners of the estate were given permission to build their own church on condition that it was disguised as a house. In 1786, the large Palladian-style 'house'

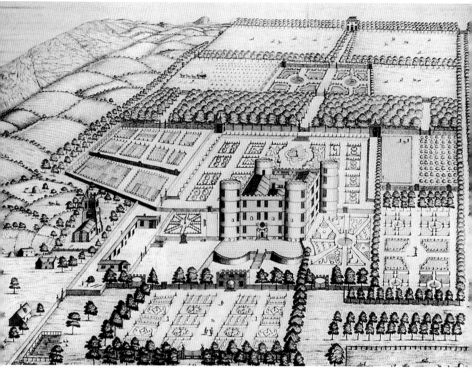

Contemporary topographical prints are scarce, which is why this one of East Lulworth is of great interest. Drawn by Margaret Weld in 1721, the landscape is full of activity, both inside and outside the park walls. The parish church alone survived the removal of the village.

was completed, the first free-standing Roman Catholic church to be erected in England since the Reformation.

John Fitzgerald Pennie (1782-1848), a native of East Lulworth, writing as Sylvaticus in his autobiographical *Tale of a Modern Genius* repopulated the empty acres around the isolated church. 'The poet of antiquarian lore', Pennie conjured up 'a bygone world, the relics of which are dust, [but] live again in the glowing colours of imagination'.

At Iwerne Stepleton, the dog-leg course of the modern road follows the western boundary of Stepleton House, diverted away from its original route which took a more direct line close to the house. It may be apocryphal but it is said that Peter Beckford was the last to tolerate such an intrusion into his privacy and invited the Highway Commissioners to dinner. After plying them with drink he called, 'Gentlemen, we are forgetting our business. Here is your [wayleave] agreement. I have made a few trifling alterations with which I need not trouble you now. Come, let us sign our names to it'. The next day the Commissioners discovered the line of the new road to which they, in their befuddled state, had agreed!

The house, reputed to occupy the site of the old village which had become deserted by 1662, stands next to the eleventh-century church of St Mary which was adapted in 1809 by Peter Beckford as a family burial vault. In 1879 Thomas Hardy's sister Mary attended a service in the chapel and described its 'very queer quire. It consists only of a shoemaker who plays the bass-viol, and his mother who sings the air'. In the grounds of the house, a rockery of masonry, locally called 'the parson's mound', is believed to be the remains of the former parsonage.

A combination of fieldwork and map analysis at Kingston Russell has shown that despite a period of decline in the sixteenth century, at least nine cottages of the medieval village survived to the east of the manor house until the turn of the eighteenth century. The building of Kingston Russell House in the late sixteenth and early seventeenth centuries by the Michels had halted the decline, but nineteenth-century landscaping removed the last vestiges of the village.

TANKS, TEMPESTS AND TOWNS

In December 1943 the Purbeck village of Tyneham was evacuated as the tanks of the Royal Armoured Corps moved in to practise live firing during the Second World War. Despite Sir Winston Churchill's pledge of restitution, the villagers have not been allowed to return and the valley remains deserted. A notice pinned to the church door as evacuation was completed reads: 'Please treat the church and houses with care. We have given up our homes, where many of us have lived

Tyneham, a village 'lost' in the twentieth century. In the late nineteenth century the village street, looking towards the church of St Mary, was a hive of activity. Today, the house walls are mere stumps – a half-way stage between humps and bumps and standing buildings.

for generations, to help win the war to keep men free. We shall return one day and thank you for treating the village kindly'.

Today only the church and schoolroom survive intact. Roofless stubs of house walls line the village street, and Tyneham House stands derelict.

The Army firing ranges extend over 7,500 acres, with restricted public access allowed at advertised times. When the villagers left Tyneham, horse and cart and small Ferguson tractors worked the fields. In a bizarre twist, and despite the bomb craters, as with large areas of Salisbury Plain which suffer the same bombardment, the pre-1940s landscape has been spared the depredation of modern farm machinery.

Access is prohibited but the Royal Commission survey of the parish shows how the Army's presence has in fact helped to preserve an ancient landscape. Domesday Book lists four places called Tyneham, which can be identified as Tyneham itself, Baltington Farm, and North and South Egliston Farms. All were in existence by the late eleventh century, centred within their own blocks of land the field boundaries of which can still be traced across the valley.

Baltington and North Egliston survive today as farms, but there are extensive earthwork remains of houses and gardens to suggest they were once hamlets. At North Egliston 'Chapel Close' is traditionally the site of a chapel dedicated to St Margaret, but by 1860 the hamlet had shrunk to only one farm and two cottages.

International conflict over the centuries has played a part in the demise of other coastal settlements. West Bexington could be seen as a failure in two phases of its history. In the 1930s attempts were made to develop it as a seaside resort with chalets, bungalows and car parking. Its present prosperity, certainly during the summer months, seems assured, and recent development has uncovered evidence for its first incarnation.

According to Thomas Gerard, writing in 1620, the village was burnt by the French in 1440 when the inhabitants were abducted and 'forced to redeem themselves at a great price . . . sithence it hath been converted to a Farme, for want of inhabitants'.

Aerial photographs confirm that the nucleus of the medieval village lay to the south and east of the complex of buildings at Manor Farm,

The destructive force of storms and high seas was unleashed on the old church at East Fleet, destroyed in November 1824 when Chesil Bank was breached and villagers ran for their lives.

bordering a medieval road leading to the sea. A parish in its own right, West Bexington once had a chapel dedicated to St Giles, before the living was united with Puncknowle in 1451 'on account of an enemy assault'. The site of the medieval church and graveyard were confirmed by excavations in 1983-4. Levelling of the area during the construction of an army vehicle park in the 1939-45 war had destroyed much of the site, but sufficient survived to pinpoint the south-east corner of the chancel.

Storms have also played their part in destroying village communities. The most memorable was that of November 1824 which battered the whole of the south coast causing the sea to break through the Chesil Bank. Hurricane force winds combined with one of the highest spring tides of the year to leave a trail of devastation, with over 100 dead, many of them lost at sea.

The eyewitness account of James Bowring, parish clerk of Fleet, as told by his son, records the ferocity and power of the hurricane. 'The sea began to break over the beach at 5 a.m. the water came up as fast as a horse could gallop. James watched as long as he dared, and then, terrified, ran for his life to Chickerell. The nave of the church was undermined and demolished, also a cottage hard by and another at the end of Butter Street. Two cottages near the garden of the old Priest's house were also thrown down. Two old ladies living in the Priest's house were rescued from a bedroom window. A hayrick was swept away and seven large fishing boats were washed far inland'.

The chancel of the old church at Fleet survives, with the new church built on higher ground at the sole expense of the rector George Gould in 1827-9. Fleet has a further claim to ecclesiastical interest in being only one of ten churches recorded in Domesday Book. Its other point of notoriety is as the setting for Meade Falkner's novel *Moonfleet*, when the vaults of the Mohun family tomb provided a hiding place for the smugglers' kegs.

The weather may not have had such a devastating effect as it did at Fleet, but the villagers of Stanton St Gabriel endured its ferocity until the 1800s. The parish church now stands at Morecombelake, whilst its predecessor is in ruins, beached like a shipwreck on the coast at the foot of Golden Cap. The sea may have provided a livelihood for some of the villagers but over time it was also a source of destruction, the unstable cliffs and coastal erosion making access increasingly difficult. The old coach road from Dorchester to Exeter used to run through the village but by 1824 traffic was using the new turnpike road to the north through Chideock and Morecombelake.

The church was a chapelry of Whitchurch Canonicorum, and Hutchins records that in 1650 the inhabitants made a plea for a settled minister for their church on the grounds that 'they seldom could repair to any other church in winter because of the violence of the wind and weather'. There were reports that 'in Mr Goforth's time [vicar of Whitchurch Canonicorum 1805-1839] the Chapel of Stanton St Gabriel was frequently used as a receiving house for smuggled kegs'.

In 1841 a new church was built at Morecombelake and by 1883 the font and chancel screen had been transferred from the old church. The village declined and the centre of activity gravitated north towards the main road, leaving the ruins of the church, a farmhouse, and cottage.

And finally, spare a thought for the 'lost' villages which have disappeared in the nineteenth and twentieth centuries, swallowed up by the urban sprawl of suburbia around the towns of Weymouth, Poole, Bournemouth, Bridport and Wareham. Today in Weymouth all that remains of the medieval village of Radipole is the small thirteenth-century church and manor house and a large field, to the west of the church, deeply carved into mounds and hollows, aptly known as Humpty Dumpty Field. The growth in popularity of the spa town has resulted in the engulfing of the former medieval parishes of Broadwey, Preston, Upwey and Wyke Regis; and the town of Melcombe Regis.

Poole now incorporates the former parishes of Branksome, Hamworthy, Longfleet, Parkstone and Canford Magna; whilst Allington with its parish church dedicated to St Swithun is now part of Bridport.

PLACES TO VISIT

Sites are vulnerable, susceptible to both human attack and natural erosion. Of those within the county, less than twenty are scheduled as Ancient Monuments by English Heritage, enjoying a measure of legal protection. Please treat all with equal care, and respect property ownership. All are on private land and a reference to a site does not imply public access.

Lost villages, 'open' to the public, courtesy of the landowner: Bardolfeston (Puddletown, SY 7694); Tyneham (with restrictions on time and access, SY 8880).

An isolated church will immediately beg the question, where was the village? In addition, earthworks indicating lost villages and areas of shrinkage within surviving villages can be viewed from an adjacent churchyard, road, bridleway, or footpath at: Dewlish (SY 7798); East Hemsworth (Witchampton, ST 9706); Holworth (Chaldon Herring SY 7783); Knowlton (Woodlands, SU 0110); Melcombe Horsey (ST 7402); Bingham's Melcombe (ST 7702); Milton Abbas (SY 8082); Modbury (Swyre, SY 5189); Radipole (SY 6681); Rew (Winterborne St Martin, SY 6389); Silton (ST 7829); Stanton St Gabriel (SY 4092); West Burton (Winfrith Newburgh, SY 8285); West Ringstead (Osmington, SY 7481); Whitcombe (SY 7188); Winterborne Farringdon (SY 6988); Winterborne Came (SY 7088); and Witchampton (ST 9806).

FURTHER READING

To appreciate the 'lost' villages of Dorset one must first read of the villages which are the survivors, and there is no better guide and companion than Jo Draper's *Dorset: The Complete Guide*, 1986).

The compilation of this small volume has relied upon the research of many individuals, whose work is published in a wide variety of sources. There are too many to list in full, but the following few will hopefully lead to the greater whole.

Aston, M., *Interpreting the Landscape*, 1985
Aston, M. & Lewis, C., (eds) *The Medieval Landscape of Wessex*, 1994
Beaton, D., *Dorset Maps*, 2001
Beresford, M. W., *The Lost Villages of England*, 1954
Beresford, M. W. & Hurst, J. G., (eds) *Deserted Medieval Villages*, 1971
Bettey, J. H., *Dorset*, 1974
    The Suppression of the Monasteries in the West Country, 1989
    'Discover Dorset' *Farming*, 2000
Bond, I., *Tyneham: A Lost Heritage*, 1956
Chaplin, C., *Dorset from the Air*, 1985
Drew, C. D., 'The Manors of the Iwerne Valley', *Proceedings of the Dorset Natural History and Archaeological Society*, vol. 69, 45-50, 1948
Good, R., *The Lost Villages of Dorset*, 1979
Groube, L. M. & Bowden, M. C. B., *The Archaeology of Rural Dorset*, Dorset Natural History and Archaeological Society, Monograph 4, 1982
Hall, T., 'Witchampton: Village Origins', *Proceedings of the Dorset Natural History and Archaeological Society*, vol. 115, 121-132, 1993
    Minster Churches in the Dorset Landscape, British Archaeological Reports 304, 2000
Hunt, A. W., *Dorset (Fieldwork)*, in *Medieval Village Research Group*, 31st *Annual Report*, 6-8, 1983
    'Woolcombe Farm', *Proceedings of the Dorset Natural History and Archaeological Society*, vol. 106, 155-9, 1984
Hutchins, J., *The History and Antiquities of the County of Dorset*, 4 vols, 1861-70
Keen, L. & Carreck, A., (eds) *Historic Landscape of the Weld Estate, Dorset*, 1987

Lock, P. W., *The Deserted Medieval Sites of Dorset*, Mansel-Pleydell Competition, manuscript deposited in Dorset County Museum, 1970

Meekings, C. A. F., *Dorset Hearth Tax Assessments*, 1951

Mills, A. D., *Dorset Place-Names; their origins and meanings*, 1986
The Dorset Lay Subsidy Roll of 1332, Dorset Record Society, vol. 4, 1971

Rahtz, P., 'Holworth Excavations', *Proceedings of Dorset Natural History and Archaeological Society*, vol. 81, 127-47, 1959

Royal Commission on Historical Monuments, Dorset, Vol I, (West); II, 1970 (South-East); III, 1970 (Central); IV, 1972 (North); V, 1975 (North-East), 1952

Taylor, C., *The Making of the English Landscape: Dorset*, 1970
Village and Farmstead, 1983
'The Regular Village Plan: Dorset revisited and revised', in *The Medieval Landscape of Wessex,* (eds. M. Aston & C. Lewis), 213-8, 1994
'Dorset and beyond', in *Making English Landscapes*, (eds. K. Barker & T. C. Darvill), 9-25, 1997

Thorn, C. & F., *Domesday Book: Dorset,* 1983

Wright, P., *The Village that Died for England*, 1995

ACKNOWLEDGEMENTS

My greatest debt is to all those who have spent far more time than I in the study of lost villages, both nationally and within the county of Dorset. By selecting any one book from the list of Further Reading the reader will begin to appreciate the intricate web that threads its way between the work that has been completed, and the opportunities for further study.

In the 1930s, Colonel C. D. Drew was the first to draw attention to the complex pattern of settlements in the Iwerne valley, and the need to identify the boundaries of the early estates and manors. In recent years his research has been augmented by the staff of the Royal Commission on Historical Monuments (now part of English Heritage), staff of the Sites and Monuments Record of Dorset County Council, individual fieldworkers such as Christopher Taylor, C.J. Bailey, Peter Lock and Alan Hunt, and students at the former Dorset Institute of Archaeology (now Bournemouth University) and the former Bristol University Extra-Mural Department.

My own reading and desk-bound study has been guided by staff at the National Monuments Record (English Heritage) in Swindon, and staff at the County Sites and Monuments Record of Dorset County Council in Dorchester. The archivists, librarians and curators at the Dorset Record Office, the Dorset County Library and the Dorset County Museum in Dorchester have directed my steps around the tip of the iceberg. In return for house-sitting, the private library of two Dorchester residents was open at all hours – thank you, Jo and Christopher. And to my husband, David, thank you for sharing the excitement (and frustration) of peering over countless hedges in the hope of spotting an elusive earthwork (no trespassing allowed).

I am grateful to all of the following for allowing the inclusion of illustrations in their possession or for which they hold the copyright: Victor Ambrus; pages 37 and 38: Cambridge University Collection of Air Photographs; pages 9, 41 and 45: Dorset County Museum; pages 61 and 69: Dorset Record Office; page 19: The Dovecote Press; pages 4, 11, 14, 20, 33, 36, 65, 67, 71: Kitchenhams Limited, Photographers; pages 35 and 58: Francesca Radcliffe; pages 12, 18, 29, 44, 49, 50, 51, 52, 60: Royal Commission for Historical Monuments (England); frontispiece, pages 21, 24, 25, 26, 39, 42, 56, 57, 63. Christopher Chaplin drew the map on page 6 and the plans on pages 22 and 47.

INDEX

The

DISCOVER DORSET

Series of Books

A series of paperback books providing informative illustrated
introductions to Dorset's history, culture and way of life.
The following titles have so far been published.

BLACKMORE VALE *Hilary Townsend*
BRIDGES *David McFetrich and Jo Parsons*
CASTLES & FORTS *Colin Pomeroy*   COAST & SEA *Sarah Welton*
CRANBORNE CHASE *Desmond Hawkins*
DOWNS, MEADOWS & PASTURES *Jim White*
DRESS & TEXTILES *Rachel Worth*
FARMHOUSES & COTTAGES *Michael Billett*
FARMING *J.H.Bettey*   FOLLIES *Jonathan Holt*
FOSSILS *Richard Edmonds*   GEOLOGY *Paul Ensom*
THE GEORGIANS *Jo Draper*   HEATHLANDS *Lesley Haskins*
THE INDUSTRIAL PAST *Peter Stanier*
ISLE OF PURBECK *Paul Hyland*   LEGENDS *Jeremy Harte*
LOST VILLAGES *Linda Viner*   MILLS *Peter Stanier*
PORTLAND *Stuart Morris*   POTTERY *Penny Copland-Griffiths*
THE PREHISTORIC AGE *Bill Putnam*
RAILWAY STATIONS *Mike Oakley*
REGENCY, RIOT & REFORM *Jo Draper*
RIVERS & STREAMS *John Wright*   THE ROMANS *Bill Putnam*
SAXONS & VIKINGS *David Hinton*   SHIPWRECKS *Maureen Attwooll*
STONE QUARRYING *Jo Thomas*   TUDORS & STUARTS *J.H. Bettey*
THE VICTORIANS *Jude James*   WOODLANDS *Anne Horsfall*

All the books about Dorset published by The Dovecote Press
are available in bookshops throughout the county,
or in case of difficulty direct from the publishers.
The Dovecote Press Ltd, Stanbridge,
Wimborne Minster, Dorset BH21 4JD
Tel: 01258 840549 www.dovecotepress.com